LIVING WITH DYSLEXIA

Beginners Approach To Combating Learning Difficulties

VINCENT JERRY

Table of Contents

Introductory

Despite having ordinary to above-average intelligence and adequate educational opportunities, dyslexia is a neurodevelopmental disorder that affects a person's ability to read, write, and spell.

It is a condition that affects a person's ability to comprehend and recognize written language throughout their lifetime. Dyslexia is a specific difficulty in processing phonological information, which is the ability to recognize and manipulate the sounds of spoken language.

It is not related to a lack of intellect, vision problems, or a lack of effort in learning to read.

Common dyslexia characteristics and symptoms may include:

• Difficulties with reading accuracy: People with dyslexia frequently struggle with word recognition and frequently misinterpret or have trouble decoding unfamiliar words.

• Slow reading speed: Individuals with dyslexia may read slowly and laboriously because they require more time to comprehend and decode written text.

• Poor spelling and writing skills: Dyslexia can also impair a person's ability to correctly spell words and communicate in writing.

• Phonological awareness is the capacity to recognize and manipulate the individual sounds (phonemes) in spoken language. People with dyslexia may struggle with rhyming, segmenting sounds within words, and blending sounds to create words.

• Challenges with fluency: Reading fluently, or effortlessly, can be challenging for individuals with dyslexia, as they may struggle with word recognition and decoding.

- Difficulties with reading comprehension: Although dyslexia predominantly affects decoding and word recognition, it can also impact reading comprehension, as individuals may expend a great deal of cognitive effort decoding words, leaving them with less mental capacity to comprehend the content.

It is important to observe that dyslexia exists on a spectrum, with varying degrees of severity between individuals. Early intervention and appropriate educational support can significantly aid those with dyslexia in developing strategies to surmount their reading and writing difficulties. To facilitate learning and enhance reading skills, these interventions may include specialized reading programs, individualized instruction, and assistive technologies. Many individuals with dyslexia can live fruitful and fulfilling lives if they receive the proper support and accommodations.

CHAPTER ONE
Indications And Symptoms

The manifestation and severity of the signs and symptoms of dyslexia can vary between individuals. It is important to remember that not all individuals with dyslexia will exhibit all of these symptoms, and the presence of one or more of these indicators does not inherently confirm a dyslexia diagnosis.

A qualified professional, such as a psychologist or educational specialist, should conduct a thorough evaluation to make a diagnosis. Therefore, the following are some prevalent signs and symptoms of dyslexia:

1. Problems with Reading:

• Slow or erroneous interpretation.

• Frequent word inversions (for example, reading "b" as "d").

• Difficulty identifying frequent sight words.

• Struggles with deciphering unknown terms.

• Fluency issues with reading.

2. Spelling Difficulties:

• Numerous spelling mistakes, including phonetic spelling.

• Trouble recalling and applying spelling standards.

• Spelling patterns that do not conform to a standard.

3. Phonological Challenges:

• Trouble distinguishing and manipulating individual sounds within words (phonological awareness).

• Difficulties with word rhyme, merging sounds, and segmenting sounds.

• Difficulty recognizing syllables.

4. Problems with Writing:

• Unprofessional calligraphy.

• Limited written communication.

• Use of inconsistent punctuation and grammar.

5. Reading Comprehension Difficulties:

• Difficulty comprehending and remembering what has been read.

• Difficulty deriving inferences and conclusions from text.

• Difficulty summarizing and explaining the content of the reading.

6. Problems with Spoken Language:

• May struggle with expressive and receptive language abilities.

• Struggles with word retrieval and conversational word selection.

• Difficulty adhering to multistep instructions.

7. Sluggish Processor Speed:

• May take longer than peers to complete reading and writing tasks.

8. To avoid reading and writing:

• Due to frustration or embarrassment, individuals with

dyslexia may avoid reading and writing duties.

9.   Low   Self-Esteem   and Nervousness:

• Difficulties associated with dyslexia can result in feelings of low self-esteem, frustration, and anxiety regarding school and academic responsibilities.

10. Family Record:

• Dyslexia frequently runs in families; therefore, a familial history of reading difficulties may be a factor to consider.

Early identification of dyslexia and provision of appropriate interventions and support are crucial. Individuals can develop strategies to surmount their reading and writing difficulties and gain confidence in their abilities through early intervention.

If you suspect that you or someone you know may have dyslexia, you should consult a qualified professional to determine the most effective course of action and support.

Neurological Basis Of Reading Impairment

Dyslexia has a complex neurological basis involving disparities in brain structure and function.

Neuroimaging techniques, such as functional magnetic resonance imaging (fMRI) and structural brain scanning, have yielded important insights into the brain regions and processes associated with dyslexia. The following are significant findings concerning the neurological basis of dyslexia.

1. Patterns of Brain Activation Differ:

- fMRI studies have revealed that individuals with dyslexia exhibit different brain activation patterns during reading tasks than those without dyslexia.

Specifically, they may exhibit less activation in regions of the brain typically associated with reading, such as the left hemisphere's posterior part, including the left temporoparietal and left occipitotemporal regions.

2. Deficits in Phonological Processing:

• Dyslexia is firmly linked to difficulties in phonological processing, which is the ability to identify and manipulate the individual sounds (phonemes) in spoken language.

Neuroimaging studies have revealed that individuals with dyslexia may have less activation in the left inferior frontal gyrus and the left superior temporal gyrus, which are areas essential for phonological processing.

3. Structure-Based Brain Variations:

• According to a number of studies, individuals with dyslexia may have structural distinctions in the brain, including alterations in the size and connectivity of specific brain regions.

These distinctions are frequently observed in regions of the brain associated with language processing, such as the arcuate fasciculus, a white matter tract connecting language-related brain regions.

4. Hereditary and Genetic Factors:

• Dyslexia has a significant genetic component, and multiple genes have been linked to its development. These genes are associated with reading-related neural pathway formation and brain development. Research indicates that individuals with a family history of dyslexia are more likely to develop the disorder.

5. Plasticity of the Brain and Intervention:

• It is essential to note that the brain is highly plastic, and that dyslexic individuals can benefit from targeted interventions and educational strategies. Changes in brain activation patterns and enhanced reading skills can result from interventions that are effective. These alterations are frequently associated with increased activity in reading-related brain regions.

6. Cognitive Adjustment:

• Some people with dyslexia develop compensatory strategies in order to manage their reading difficulties. These strategies may involve employing various brain regions or cognitive processes to surmount obstacles, highlighting the brain's adaptability.

It is essential to emphasize that dyslexia is not caused by sloth, a lack of effort, or poor instruction. It is a neurobiological disorder that effects the brain's ability to process written language.

Individuals with dyslexia can develop effective reading strategies and realize their maximum potential if they are identified and treated promptly.

Researchers continue to investigate the neurological basis of dyslexia in an effort to enhance our understanding of the disorder and develop more effective interventions and support.

CHAPTER TWO
Impact On Education And Living

Dyslexia can have a significant impact on a person's learning and daily life, but with the proper support and interventions, people with dyslexia can achieve success and live fulfilling lives. Here are a few ways in which dyslexia can impact learning and daily life, as well as strategies for mitigating its effects:

1. Academic Difficulties:

• Dyslexia predominantly impacts reading, writing, and spelling abilities, which can have an effect on academic performance.

Individuals with dyslexia may have difficulty with reading comprehension, essay writing, and penmanship tests.

- Individuals with dyslexia can develop strong reading and writing skills with the assistance of specialized educational interventions, such as structured literacy programs. Teachers and parents can provide additional assistance and accommodations, such as extended testing time, audiobooks, and assistive technology.

2. Inadequate Self-Esteem and Frustration:

• Difficulties associated with dyslexia can result in feelings of frustration, low self-esteem, and anxiety, particularly in educational contexts where reading and writing are emphasized.

• It is essential to provide emotional support and encouragement to individuals with dyslexia as a mitigation strategy. Developing self-assurance and resiliency is crucial. Students' self-esteem can also be boosted by recognizing and praising their strengths and abilities in areas besides literacy.

3. Social and Emotional Repercussions:

• Dyslexia can have a negative impact on social interactions and self-esteem. Children with dyslexia may feel different from their classmates and are susceptible to bullying and teasing.

• Individuals with dyslexia can navigate social challenges with the assistance of a positive self-image and a supportive environment at home and in the classroom. Encourage open communication and teach self-advocacy skills to assist them in communicating their requirements.

4. Professional and Employment Difficulties:

• Dyslexia can continue to impact a person's profession, as many occupations require reading and writing. Individuals with dyslexia take longer to complete written work or reports.

• Success can be achieved by identifying strengths and pursing careers that align with those strengths. Additionally, seeking workplace accommodations such as assistive technology or additional time for written tasks can help individuals with dyslexia excel in their careers.

5. Lifelong Education:

• Dyslexia does not disappear with age, but individuals can learn strategies to overcome their difficulties and improve their reading and writing abilities throughout their lives.

• Individuals with dyslexia can benefit from lifelong learning and the use of assistive technology. Many individuals with dyslexia achieve success in postsecondary education by utilizing academic support and accommodations.

6. Competencies and abilities:

• It is essential to acknowledge that individuals with dyslexia frequently possess distinctive strengths and abilities, such as creativity, problem-solving skills, and strong visual thinking abilities.

• Individuals' confidence and sense of self-worth can be enhanced through the encouragement of the development of these strengths and the provision of opportunities to investigate and excel in areas of interest.

Overall, despite the fact that dyslexia can present difficulties, early diagnosis and appropriate interventions can substantially mitigate its effects. Individuals with dyslexia can realize their full potential and lead successful, fulfilling lives if they receive support from educators and family members and employ effective strategies and accommodations.

Educational Methodologies

Individuals with dyslexia require effective educational strategies to develop strong reading and writing skills, create self-confidence, and achieve academic success. These strategies should be tailored to the specific requirements and strengths of each individual. Here are some educational strategies and approaches that can be beneficial for dyslexic students:

1. Programs for Structured Literacy Instruction:

• Structured literacy programs are evidence-based approaches that teach reading and writing fundamentals in a systematic manner. Typically, explicit instruction is provided in phonemic awareness, phonics, vocabulary, comprehension, and penmanship. The Orton-Gillingham method is an example of a well-known structured literacy program.

2. Multisensory Instruction:

• Multisensory techniques utilize multiple modalities (e.g., visual, auditory, kinesthetic) to facilitate learning. For example, students might use colored sandpaper letters or engage in activities that involve tracing letters while saying their corresponding noises.

3. Activities for Awareness of Phonetics:

• An understanding of phonology is essential for reading success. This skill can be enhanced through activities that emphasize alliteration, segmenting sounds in words, and blending sounds to form words.

4. Explicit Instruction in Phonetics:

• Provide explicit, systematic instruction in phonology, including the correspondence between letters and their associated sounds. This helps students precisely decode words.

5. Regular Reading Exercises:

• Encourage consistent reading practice to improve reading fluency and comprehension. Permit students to peruse materials at their reading level to build their confidence.

6. Books on tape and assistive technology:

- Audiobooks, text-to-speech and speech-to-text software can assist students in accessing and comprehending written materials. Additionally, these instruments can alleviate the annoyance associated with reading difficulties.

7. Additional Time for Assignments and Exams:

- Offer extended time for completing assignments to enable students with dyslexia to work at their own pace and decrease time strain.

8. Individualized Learning:

• Recognize that each dyslexic learner is unique. When necessary, provide individual or small-group instruction that is tailored to their particular requirements.

9. Visual Assistances:

• Graphic organizers, visual schedules, and color-coding can help students organize their thoughts and information.

10. Reinforcement and encouragement that is positive:

• Offer constructive feedback and encouragement to enhance self-esteem and motivation. Celebrate the accomplishments of pupils, no matter how small.

11. Self-Advocate Abilities:

• Teach students self-advocacy skills so they can communicate their needs to instructors and request assistance or accommodations as needed.

12. Collaboration with Service Support:

• Develop and implement individualized education plans (IEPs) or 504 plans that address the specific requirements of the student with dyslexia in close collaboration with special education professionals, reading specialists, and speech therapists.

13. Continuing Education for Educators:

• Ensure that instructors receive training and professional development in dyslexia awareness and effective teaching strategies for students with dyslexia.

14. Parental Participation:

- Involve parents in their child's education, provide resources and guidance on how to support their child's learning at home, and maintain an open line of communication with parents.

It is essential to note that early intervention is essential for effectively addressing dyslexia. The sooner dyslexia is identified and appropriate interventions are implemented, the better the individual's outcomes will be.

Additionally, a supportive and empathetic learning environment is essential for assisting students with dyslexia succeed academically and develop self-confidence.

CHAPTER THREE
Interventions For Dyslexia

Interventions for dyslexia seek to provide individuals with effective strategies and support to enhance their reading, writing, and spelling abilities, as well as their academic and emotional well-being as a whole.

These interventions should be tailored to each person's specific requirements and may include a combination of educational, therapeutic, and assistive approaches.

Here are some common interventions for dyslexia:

1. Programs for Structured Literacy Instruction:

• Research-based structured literacy programs, such as the Orton-Gillingham approach, Wilson Reading System, and Lindamood-Bell programs, provide systematic instruction in phonological awareness, phonology, fluency, vocabulary, and comprehension.

2. Training in Phonological Awareness:

• Phonological awareness exercises emphasize the development of a person's ability to recognize and manipulate spoken language sounds. These activities may include rhyming, sound synthesis, sound segmentation, and syllable manipulation.

3. Phonics Education:

• Explicit phonics instruction teaches the correspondence between letters and the sounds they represent. It helps individuals precisely decode words and develop spelling skills.

4. Multisensory Strategies:

• Multisensory methods utilize multiple modalities (e.g., visual, auditory, kinesthetic) to reinforce learning. For instance, students could trace sandpaper letters while pronouncing the associated sounds.

5. Helpful Technology:

• Assistive technology tools, such as text-to-speech software, speech-to-text software, and specialized typefaces, can facilitate easier access to written materials for individuals with dyslexia.

6. Books on tape and recorded texts:

• Providing access to audiobooks and recorded texts enables individuals with reading difficulties to access and appreciate literature and educational materials.

7. Individualized Education Program (IEP) and Section 504 Plans:

• Schools can develop individualized programs outlining specific accommodations and support for dyslexic students. These plans may include extended time for homework and exams, preferred seating, and access to specialized literacy instruction.

8. Language and Speech Therapy:

• Speech therapists can help people with dyslexia improve their language and articulation abilities, which can have a positive effect on their reading and spelling.

9. Individual or small-group tutoring with reading and writing specialists can provide individualized instruction and targeted support.

10. Psychotherapy and emotional support:

• Emotional support from school counselors or psychologists can assist individuals with dyslexia in coping with any tension, anxiety, or self-esteem issues that may arise as a result of their learning difficulties.

11. Parental Participation:

• Parents can play a vital role in their child's development by collaborating closely with teachers, providing a supportive home environment, and participating in activities that promote reading and language abilities.

12. Continuing Education:

• Interventions for dyslexia are not restricted to childhood only. Adults and adolescents with dyslexia can benefit from ongoing support, such as tutoring, assistive technology, and workplace and higher education accommodations.

It is essential to observe that dyslexia interventions should be based on evidence and administered by trained professionals.

Early intervention, individualized support, and a collaborative approach involving instructors, parents, and specialists are crucial for assisting individuals with dyslexia to overcome their challenges and succeed in their academic and extracurricular endeavors.

Providing Assistance To Dyslexic Individuals

Supporting dyslexic individuals entails creating an environment that is inclusive and accommodating, recognizing their unique needs and strengths. Whether you are a teacher, parent, friend, or colleague, here are some methods to assist those with dyslexia.

1. Raise Awarenes and Comprehension:

• Educate yourself and others about dyslexia in order to dispel myths and increase awareness of the condition. This can aid in stigma reduction and cultivate empathy.

2. Early Recognition and Evaluation:

• If you suspect a child has dyslexia, request an evaluation as soon as possible from a qualified professional. Intervention at an early stage is crucial for effective support.

3. Customized Educational Assistance:

• In educational settings, collaborate with educators to develop and implement individualized education plans

(IEPs) or 504 plans outlining specific accommodations and interventions to meet the requirements of the student.

4. Programs for Structured Literacy Instruction:

• Promote the use of structured literacy programs that provide systematic and explicit reading, writing, and grammar instruction. These programs founded on evidence can be extremely effective.

5. Helpful Technology:

• Encourage the use of assistive technology tools, such as text-to-speech software and speech-to-text applications, to facilitate easier access to written materials.

6. Books on tape and accessible materials:

• Make accessible materials and audiobooks available to individuals with dyslexia so that they can access and appreciate literature and educational content.

7. Positive encouragement and support:

• Provide praise and positive reinforcement for their efforts and achievements, regardless of their size. Self-esteem building is crucial.

8. Adaptability and Tenacity:

• Recognize that dyslexic people may require additional time to complete reading and writing duties. Be patient and make the necessary adjustments.

9. Individualized Education Programs:

• Tailor teaching methods to the strengths and requirements of each student. Determine and develop their talents and interests.

10. Multisensory Instruction:

• Promote the use of multisensory learning strategies that engage multiple senses to reinforce learning.

11. Activities for Awareness of Phonetics:

•	Encourage phonological awareness-improving activities, such as rhyming games and word segmentation exercises.

12. Develop Self-Advocacy Abilities:

• Teach individuals with dyslexia how to advocate for themselves by communicating their needs and, when necessary, seeking assistance or accommodations.

13. Emotional Assistance:

• Create a secure and supportive environment where individuals feel comfortable discussing their dyslexia-related challenges and emotions. Deal with any prospective frustration, anxiety, or low self-esteem.

14. Promote Talents and Passions:

• Encourage dyslexic individuals to discover and cultivate their strengths and passions, which can enhance their self-esteem and sense of self-worth.

15. Inclusive Methodologies:

• Promote inclusive practices in schools and workplaces to guarantee the full inclusion of individuals with dyslexia in educational and professional settings.

16. Professional Progress:

• Encourage teachers and educators to receive training and professional development in effective teaching strategies and dyslexia awareness.

17. Proponents of Accessibility:

• Advocate for accessibility in educational materials, workplace policies, and public spaces to ensure equal access to information and opportunities for individuals with dyslexia.

Supporting dyslexic individuals necessitates collaboration between family members, educators, and employers, as well as the larger community. By creating an inclusive and supportive environment and implementing evidence-based strategies, we can assist those with dyslexia to thrive and realize their complete potential.

The Conclusion

Regardless of intellect or educational opportunities, dyslexia is a neurodevelopmental disorder that affects a person's ability to read, write, and spell.

It is a lifelong disorder with a neurological basis, characterized by phonological processing difficulties and other difficulties. However, with the proper interventions and support, people with dyslexia can overcome these obstacles and live successful, fulfilling lives.

Structured literacy programs, phonological awareness training, assistive technology, and individualized education plans are all effective dyslexia interventions. , but:. In addition, providing emotional support, fostering an inclusive and accepting environment, and raising awareness about dyslexia are essential components of supporting dyslexic individuals.

Recognizing the strengths and abilities of individuals with dyslexia, as well as fostering their self-esteem and self-advocacy skills, are essential components of assisting them in reaching their maximum potential. They have dyslexia, but it does not determine their value or potential for success.

Collaboration among educators, parents, friends, colleagues, and the broader community is essential in the voyage of supporting dyslexic individuals. By collaborating and promoting inclusive practices, we can enable individuals with dyslexia to succeed academically and in life, while also contributing to a more compassionate and inclusive society.

THE END